# Hands on Literacy

## Liz Webster
## Linda Duncan

# Acknowledgements

The authors and publishers would like to thank the children of Aldingbourne Primary School and the Vale First School for their enthusiasm, hard work and cooperation in the making of this book. Liz Webster, Headteacher of Aldingbourne Primary school, would like to thank all of her staff for their cooperation and a particular thank you to Wendy Davies for her patience and support during the children's photo shoots. Linda Duncan would like to give thanks to Karen Harkin and Pam Jezard for their cooperation, enthusiasm and hard work. Finally they would again like to thank Steve Forest, the photographer, for his continued good humour, professionalism and his endless patience.

**Super Suitcases (page 16)**

Published by Collins, An imprint of HarperCollins*Publishers*
77 – 85 Fulham Palace Road, Hammersmith, London, W6 8JB

Browse the complete Collins catalogue at
www.collinseducation.com

© HarperCollins*Publishers* Limited 2011
Previously published in 2006 by Folens
First published in 2006 by Belair Publications

10 9 8 7 6 5 4 3 2 1

ISBN-13 978-0-00-743937-9

Liz Webster and Linda Duncan assert their moral rights to be identified as the authors of this work

British Library Cataloguing in Publication Data
A Catalogue record for this publication is available from the British Library

Every effort has been made to trace copyright holders and to obtain their permission for the use of copyright material. The authors and publishers will gladly receive any information enabling them to rectify any error or omission in subsequent editions.

Commissioning Editor: Zöe Nichols
Cover design: Mount Deluxe
Photography: Steve Forest

Editors: Gaynor Spry
Page layout: Suzanne Ward

Printed and bound by Printing Express Limited, Hong Kong

**Mixed Sources**
Product group from well-managed forests and other controlled sources
www.fsc.org Cert no. SW-COC-001806
© 1996 Forest Stewardship Council
FSC

# Contents

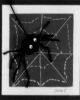

# Introduction

Welcome to *Hands on Literacy*.

As practising primary school teachers we believe that Literacy displays should be creative, purposeful, stimulating and interactive. In this book we have shown how to display Literacy ideas so that they become a valuable tool for learning as well as enriching the classroom environment.

Literacy should always be fun, practical, exciting and purposeful. This book offers a wealth of entertaining and original ideas that we use daily in our classrooms, so we know they work!

Every theme in this book follows the same basic structure by including a whole-class starter, practical ideas, art and display, and cross-curricular links.

## Whole-class Starter

This is the main focus of the theme and must be exciting, interesting and purposeful.

- 'Teacher in role' is an ideal way to stimulate the children's interest and excitement for learning. It instantly engages them and gives the lesson a purpose. We are fully aware that not all teachers are comfortable 'in role' but sometimes a crown or a cloak is enough!

- Visual props are a must and are an essential part of the whole-class starter, but they need to be big and bold.

- 'Talk partners' involves the children sharing ideas with each other. It also acts as a support for less confident children who may find it difficult to express ideas to a larger group.

- Interactive games include all learners and learning styles.

## Practical Ideas

Children love playing games and this part of the lesson reinforces what they have learned during the whole-class starter session. We have included ideas for table-top games, carpet games and large area games. All these games actively engage the children and encourage them to be excited about their learning. It is a refreshing approach to the teaching of Literacy and should replace the mundane worksheet approach.

Recording children's work is an essential part of their learning and understanding. Recording needs to be done in an imaginative way, for example, using shaped paper or shaped books, zig-zag books, posters, spiral-bound books and so on.

## Art and Display

We truly believe that bright, colourful and purposeful displays make a difference to the children's learning as well as enhancing the classroom environment. Children enjoy using their imagination and practical skills. The use of art as a tool encourages them to explore and experiment with different mediums as well as furthering their learning and understanding in Literacy.

## Cross-curricular Links

We believe that a cross-curricular approach is a more natural way for young children to learn. In this book we have made links with other curriculum areas such as Science, ICT, Design and Technology, PSHE, Music and RE. The teaching of Literacy should include:

Liveliness
Interactive teaching
Talk partners
Energy
Role play
Activity
Creativity
Yes!

Literacy is fun!

Have lots of fun and make a difference!

*Liz Webster* and *Linda Duncan*

# S is for Summer

## Whole-class Starter

- In role as the Summer Sun Queen tell the children that everything you own begins with a special letter. Ask the children to sit quietly as you produce objects that begin with the letter 's' – sunglasses, sandals, seaweed etc. Ask the children to whisper the letter, shout the letter, sing the letter and draw the letter in the air.

- Ask the children to sit in a circle and give the first child a plastic letter 's'. The child then says a word beginning with 's' and passes it to the next person.

- Play the above game but this time the children pass the 's' to music and when the music stops the child thinks of two 's' words that go together such as silly sandals, silver sunglasses etc.

### Focus of Learning

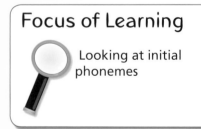

Looking at initial phonemes

## Practical Activities

- Play 'Summer Sounds'. Make a set of large laminated suns and a set of picture cards, some beginning with 's' and some beginning with other letters. Ask each child to pick a card and if it begins with 's' they write an 's' on one of the sun's rays. If it is not an 's' they put it back on the table.

- Play 'Summer Sun'. Make a set of sun cards with the letter 's' on one side and a picture of an object starting with 's' on the other. Place the cards around the classroom, hall or outside area. In small groups the children search for the suns, and when they find one they write the 's' word on a whiteboard.

- Play 'Search for the Sun'. Make a set of sunrays with pictures beginning with 's' on the back. Place the rays around the classroom, hall or outside area. In small groups the children search for the sunrays and when they find a ray they write the 's' word on the ray. Then they take the ray back to the classroom and begin to make a sun (a large yellow circle needs to be made and left on the table as a starting point). They continue to search for sunrays until a complete sun has been made (approximately eight rays).

## Art and Display

- Use chalk pastels to create giant summer pictures and display with a variety of 's' words.

- Create a sun picture by trickling PVA glue in the shape of the sun onto white calico. When dry, paint with fabric paint. Use threads and sequins to add texture to the finished piece of artwork.

## Cross-curricular Links

- **ICT** – In pairs or small groups the children decide where in the school they could find evidence of summer. For example, salvias, children wearing sandals etc. Use the digital camera to take photographs and add these to the display.

- **DRAMA** – In small groups the children make the letter 's' using their bodies. They could do this individually, in pairs or in small groups. Other letters can also be introduced.

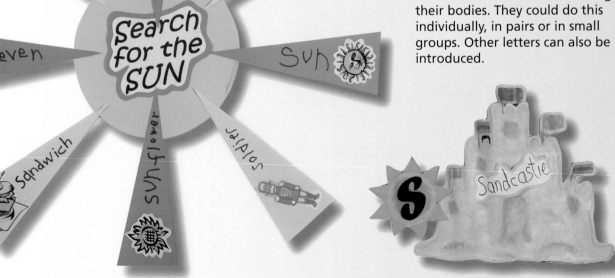

# R is for Rudolph

## Whole-class Starter

- Sing *Rudolph the Red-nosed Reindeer*. Ask the children what phoneme Rudolph begins with. Did they hear any more 'r' words? Sing again and this time ask the children to clap hands on every 'r' word.

- Play 'Rudolph Spies'. Place a selection of objects, some beginning with 'r' and some beginning with other letters around the room. Ask a child to put on some Rudolph antlers, to say "Rudolph spies something beginning with 'r'" and to choose another child to find the correct object.

## Focus of Learning

Understanding initial phonemes

## Practical Activities

- Play 'Race and Write R'. Using the picture cards from 'Race to be Rudolph' (page 9), place these around the room and ask the children to find a Rudolph card with an 'r' picture on the back. When they have found it they race back to the table and write the letter 'r' ten times on their whiteboard. An extension activity would be to try and write the whole word for the item shown on the card.

- Play 'Rudolph's Red Nose'. Make a set of boards with six Rudolph faces without noses. Make a set of red noses and make a spinner with pictures of 'r' words and not 'r' words. Give each child a board. The children take turns to spin the spinner. If it lands on an 'r' picture they place a red nose on one Rudolph face and write the letter 'r' on his nose. The object of the game is to put a red nose on each Rudolph face.

- Play 'Race to be Rudolph'. Make several sets of Rudolph outfits (antlers, a red nose, a bib with 'r' on, brown gloves, a tail and some jingle bells) and place each full outfit in a hoop. Make a set of large cards with the letter 'r' or a picture beginning with 'r', and a set of random letters and pictures. Place the cards around the room. Now ask one child to sit in each hoop and to wait for a signal. The object of the game is to pick a card and return to their hoop. If they have picked an 'r' card they put on one item such as the red nose or antlers. Repeat. The first child to be wearing all the items stands in their hoop and says, "I'm the real Rudolph!"

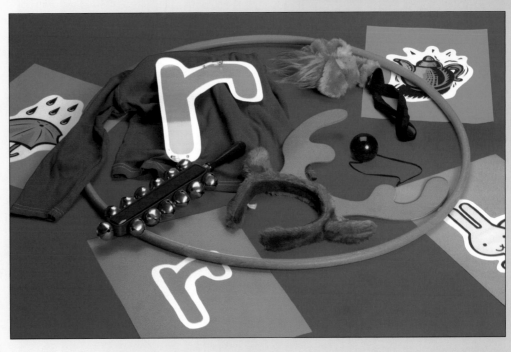

## Art and Display

- Use paint and collage material to make a large picture of Rudolph. Display this with other 'r' words. Paint individual Rudolph faces and add these to the display.

- Make a Rudolph mask using a paper plate for the face and brown hand prints for the antlers. Add a shiny red nose.

## Cross-curricular Links

- **DESIGN & TECHNOLOGY** – Design and make a Rudolph finger puppet.

- **SCIENCE** – Present the children with a problem: Rudolph's nose has broken and he needs to light it up ready for Christmas Eve. Can you help? Provide a selection of batteries and circuits.

- **PSHE** – Read or tell the story of 'Rudolph the Red-nosed Reindeer'. Talk about feelings: how Rudolph might have felt when he was excluded from the games, how Rudolph might have felt because he was different from the others.

- **MUSIC** – Sing the alternative version of *Rudolph the Red-nosed Reindeer* shown on page 72. Try this as a whole group first, then split the children into three groups. Group 1 could sing the correct version, group 2 could sing only the extra bits (e.g. 'like a light bulb'), and group 3 could play the percussion instruments. Repeat the activity, swapping the groups around.

# On the Ning Nang Nong

## Whole-class Starter

- Read and enjoy the poem 'On the Ning Nang Nong' by Spike Milligan (in *Juggling a Jug of Jelly*, OUP). Talk about the 'nonsense' element of the poem. Ask the children which words are repeated throughout the poem and display these on the board – 'ning', 'nang', 'nong', 'bong', 'clang', 'ping'. What do they notice about these words?

- Play 'Ning Nang Nong'. Make two sets of picture cards, one set containing 'wing', 'ring', 'sing', 'bang', 'fang', 'hang', 'dong', 'long', 'song', and a set with different endings such as 'path', 'sink', 'church', 'ghost' and so on. Place the cards in the middle of the circle of children. One child turns over two cards. If they rhyme, the children shout, "Ning nang nong!" and you can display the words on the board. If they don't match the children shout "Jibber jabber joo!" and another child has a turn.

## Practical Activities

- Play 'Word Detectives'. Give each child a laminated copy of the poem 'On the Ning Nang Nong', a magnifying glass and a word detective badge. Ask the children to circle all the 'ng' endings.

## Focus of Learning

Looking at 'ng' endings

- Play 'Ning Nang No, Four in a Row' (a game played in pairs). Make a four-by-four grid board for each pair of children, a set of words cards (ending in 'ng') and two sorts of counters (a teapot and a cow). Place the word cards face down on the table. Each child takes it in turns to pick a card and read the word. If the word ends in 'ng' they place a counter on the board. If not they miss a turn. The object of the game is to get four in a row.

- Give children shaped paper or make shaped books, for example, in the shape of a cow, a teapot or a tree. Ask the children to create their own nonsense rhyme. For example, 'On the Pong Ping Pang, Where the sheep go clang, And the crocodiles all go snap …'. Have fun!

## Art and Display

- Make large cows and display these with the children's own nonsense rhymes and other words that end in 'ng'.
- Draw pictures of the 'Ning Nang Nong' and use watercolours or pencil crayons to colour.

- Paint, pastel or stencil teapot designs on teapot-shaped paper and add to the display.

## Cross-curricular Links

- **MUSIC** – Use percussion to accompany 'On the Ning Nang Nong'.

- **PSHE** – Ask the children to imagine their world becomes like 'Ning Nang Nong'. What would it be like? For example, sweets hanging on trees, fizzy drinks coming out of water fountains. Discuss the implications.

# Spot the Spider

## Whole-class Starter

- As part of a topic on spiders talk about the word 'spider' and ask the children how many phonemes they can hear at the beginning of the word. Tell the children that 'sp' is a blend. Show the children a selection of pictures all beginning with 'sp', for example, 'spade', 'spanner', 'space', 'spaghetti', 'spot', 'spin', 'spoon'. Ask the children what they notice. (All these words begin with 'sp'). Can they think of any more?

- Using the word 'spider' as a stimulus, challenge the children to think of words beginning with 'sp' to describe the spider, for example, 'spooky spider', 'sporty spider', 'spinning spider', 'special spider', 'spotty spider'. Make a collection of these words.

## Practical Activities

- Play 'Spot the Spider'. Make a set of laminated cards with five spiders on for each child. Make a spinner with 'sp' on some sections and spiders on another (see picture). The children take turns to spin the spinner. If it lands on 'sp' that child writes a word beginning with 'sp'. If it lands on a spider the child shouts, "Spot the spider!" and draws a spot on his spider instead of a word. The object of the game is to see who has the least number of spotted spiders.

- Play 'I Spy the Spider'. Make a set of spider body cards and lots of legs! Use blend picture cards and place them in a basket. The children take turns to pick a card. If it is an 'sp' word they add a leg to their spider. The first complete spider wins.

- Play 'Spinning Spiders'. Give each child a laminated card with a spider's web drawn on, and a dictionary. You will also need a cotton reel with a pretend spider attached to a long thread. On the words, "Spin the spider!" the children look in their dictionaries to find 'sp' words and write them on their webs while one child reels in the spider. When the spider hits the reel the child shouts, "Spinning spiders!" and the children stop writing. Each child has a turn to reel in the spider.

## Art and Display

- Make a giant hairy spider for display using fur fabric and add this to the display board with 'sp' words.

- Ask children to design their own spider (for example, spotty spider, spooky spider, special spider) using paint and collage technique. Add these to the display.

- Use silver thread to sew a spider's web onto blue hessian. Make a pom-pom spider using black wool and attach it to the web.

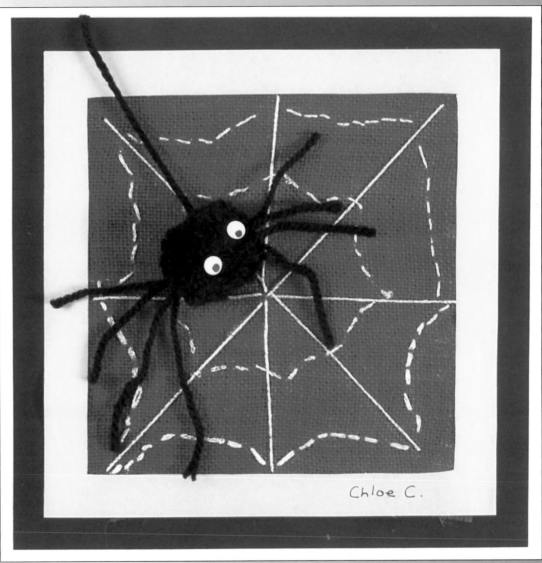

Chloe C.

## Cross-curricular Links

- **DESIGN & TECHNOLOGY** – Design and make a 3D spider.

- **SCIENCE** – Find out about spiders and make a zig-zag book of spectacular spider facts.

- **HISTORY** – Together say the nursery rhyme 'Little Miss Muffet' and think about why she might have been afraid of spiders. Find out who Miss Muffet was!

# K is for Kissing a Cool Kangaroo

## Focus of Learning

Understanding alphabetical order

## Whole-class Starter

- Read and enjoy the story *K is for Kissing a Cool Kangaroo* written by Giles Andreae, illustrated by Guy Parker-Rees (Orchard Books). Talk about alphabetical order and why it is useful. Can the children think of any times when alphabetical order is used? (For example, register, peg labels, dictionaries.)

- Play 'Pick'n'Mix'. Put all the letters of the alphabet in a bag. Ask a child to pick out five letters and to put them randomly on the board. Then ask the children to help you put the letters into alphabetical order.

- Play 'Musical ABC'. Ask the children to sit in a circle. Then place three large hoops in the middle labelled 'beginning', 'middle' and 'end'. Give each child a letter of the alphabet and ask them to decide whether their letter comes at the beginning, middle or end of the alphabet. Play some gentle music while the children place their letter in the correct hoop.

## Practical Activities

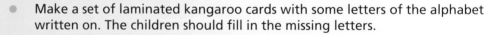

- Make a set of laminated kangaroo cards with some letters of the alphabet written on. The children should fill in the missing letters.

- Help the children to make own little alphabet books based on the story.

- Play 'Dictionary Dash'. Give each child a dictionary. Pick out a letter from a bag and prompt the children to 'dash' to the correct page. An extension would be to ask the children to write a word or two on their whiteboard beginning with that letter.

- Play 'J is for Jenga'. Stick letters of the alphabet on each brick of a set of giant jenga or large wooden blocks. Stack the bricks on the floor, ensuring that all the letters can be seen. The children take turns to pick out a letter brick *following alphabetical order* without knocking down the tower!

## Art and Display

- Paint or collage a large 'Cool Kangaroo' and add this to a display board.

- Design personalised letters. Each child chooses a letter (the initial letter of their own name would be a good idea) and draws pictures around and on the letter.

- Create illuminated letters where the children use watercolour pencils to design other letters.

- Make an alphabet collage. Help the children to cut out letter shapes or large letters from newspapers and magazines.

## Cross-curricular Links

- **ICT** – Use the digital camera to take pictures for a class alphabet book, for example, 'K is for kicking a football, H is for headteacher, M is for medical room'.

- **GEOGRAPHY / HISTORY** – Investigate other alphabets. Look at the Greek alphabet and compare it to our alphabet. Discuss with the children whether the letters are the same shape, size, sound and how many letters there are. What do they notice?

- **MATHS** – Play the game 'Maths Puzzle'. First, give each letter of the alphabet a number, for example, A is 1, B is 2 and so on. Then ask the children to find the value of a variety of words. For example, 'kangaroo' would be $11 + 1 + 14 + 7 + 1 + 18 + 15 + 15 = 82$. 'Ant' might be an easier option!

# Super Suitcases

## Focus of Learning

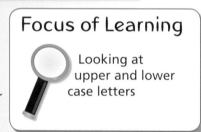

Looking at upper and lower case letters

- In role dressed to go on holiday, show the children two suitcases – one large and one small. The large suitcase should be full of a mix of capital and lower case letters and the small suitcase should contain the remainder of the alphabet in upper and lower case letters (so that the all the cards, when put together, will make up the alphabet in lower case and upper case letters).
  Ask the children to explain what they can see in the suitcases. Ask why the letters are different sizes. The children should reply that some are capital letters and some are lower case. Ask the children to help you sort the letters into the correct suitcase – capital letters in the large suitcase and lower case in the small suitcase. The children could do this activity while listening to some suitable holiday music!

- Play 'Learn Your Letters'. Give each child a whiteboard and pen. Put a mixture of capital letters and lower case letters into a bag and, as each letter is pulled out of the bag, the children write the corresponding upper or lower case letter on their white boards.

- Play 'Tops and Tails'. Explain to the children that they are going to predict which sort of letter will be pulled out of the bag. If they think it will be an upper case letter, they put their hands on their heads, and if they think it will be lower case they put their hands on their knees! To play the game the children need to be standing up. If they are correct with their prediction they remain standing, and if they are wrong they sit down!

## Practical Activities

- Play 'Fill Your Suitcase'. Make a set of suitcase-shaped bingo boards. On the boards put a selection of upper and lower case letters. Make a spinner with the words 'capital letter' and 'lower case' written on each section. On one section of the spinner put a picture of an aeroplane. The children take turns to spin the spinner and cover the appropriate letter on their board with an upper- or lower- case letter. If they land on an aeroplane they fill their board and jet away on holiday!

- Play 'Collecting Capitals'. Make a set of bingo boards with lower case letters written all over. Put corresponding capital letters in a bag and ask the children to take it turns to pull out a letter. If the capital letter corresponds to the lower case on their board they place the capital letter over the lower case letter!

- Play 'Find the Sunshine'. Make a set of suitcase-shaped laminated boards, or simply cut white paper in the shape of a suitcase. Make a set of large suns, each with a capital or lower case letter written on and place them around the school. The children then walk around the school and find the suns. When they get to a sun they write the letter that is on the sun and the corresponding upper or lower case letter on their suitcase.

## Art and Display

- Paint and collage two large suitcases and display capital letters in one and lower case letters in the other.

- Collect pebbles of different sizes and create letters in sand.

- Weave letters – an outdoor activity – using strips of plastic and a suitable mesh fence!

- Decorate cut-out upper and lower case letters in pastels.

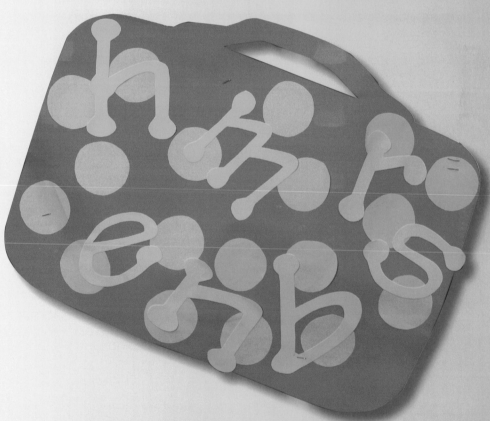

## Cross-curricular Links

- **ICT** – Put a sunhat and a pair of sunglasses on a 'Roamer' robot. Each child picks a letter and programmes Roamer to take it to the correct suitcase.

- **D&T / SCIENCE** – Make a circuit board to 'Light up the Letters'.

- **MATHS** – Create symmetrical letters. Squared paper might be useful here.

# Mr Wolf's Pancakes

## Focus of Learning

Looking at compound words

## Whole-class Starter

- In role as Mr Wolf, explain to the children that you are going to teach them how to make pancakes. Out of a bag, take a pan and some cakes and pretend to mix them in a really large bowl. Then produce two cards with 'pan' and 'cakes' written on them. Put them together to make the compound word 'pancakes' and say, "I have made some lovely pancakes". The children should say, "Oh no, you haven't!" Explain what you have done and show the children how to make 'football', 'lipstick', 'butterfly', 'snowflake' and so on with other word cards (and the objects if you have them). Explain how to make compound words.

- Play 'Mix and Match'. Make a set of cards so that when any two are put together they make a compound word (use words or pictures according to the ability of the children). Give each child a card. On a given signal, or when some gentle music is played, ask the children to find a partner to make a compound word.

- Play 'Connect a Compound'. Make a set of large jigsaw pieces with words written on each piece, such as 'pan' written on one and 'cake' written on another. Ask the children to sit in a circle and give each child a jigsaw piece. Place the corresponding pieces of puzzle on the floor in the middle of the circle. Play some gentle music and ask the children to take turns to connect the jigsaw pieces and make a compound word.

## Practical Activities

- Play 'Connect Four Compound'. Using a giant Connect Four game, stick a picture on each piece of the game. For example 'ball',' bag', 'hand', 'foot', 'stick', 'lip', 'pan', 'cake' and so on. Split the children into two teams. The object of the game is to make compound words by placing the pieces into the Connect Four frame.

- Play 'Chase It, Collect It, Connect It and Say It'. Make a set of large visual jigsaw cards so that when two are put together they make a compound word. Pin half a compound word on some of the children in the group and give the remaining children a corresponding card to hold. On a given signal the children chase each other, collect the correct card, take it off the child (carefully!) and connect it to make a compound word. Then both children should say the word.

- Play 'Spin a Compound'. Make a set of laminated bingo boards. On each board write or put a picture of a simple word that could be used to make a compound word such as 'net', 'snow', 'fire' and so on. On the spinner write or put a picture of simple corresponding words such as 'ball', 'man', 'place'. The children take turns to spin the spinner and try to make a compound word. The children can either write the word or make it with letters.

## Art and Display

- Make a large wolf and pancakes with words that can be made into compound words for display.

- In pairs, paint or pastel large jigsaw pictures of compound words.

- Collect a variety of objects to be used to create a compound sculpture. Ask the children to arrange the objects creatively and to sketch their compound sculpture. For example butter, a cup and a buttercup. Alternatively, they could write all the compound words that they can see in the sculpture on a whiteboard.

## Cross-curricular Links

- **DESIGN & TECHNOLOGY** – Make pancakes and then…

- **PHYSICAL EDUCATION** – … hold a pancake race!

- **R.E.** – Discuss Shrove Tuesday.

# Magic 'E'

## Whole-class Starter

- Marvo the Magical Magician arrives (you in role) to share his magic tricks with the children! (Use a top hat, cape and moustache!) Explain to the children that your magic will help them to spell. Put the word 'mat' into the top hat and say the magic words, "Add an 'e', a sprinkle of glee, say hee hee; What do we see?" Pull the word 'mate' out of the hat and ask the children what they notice. Explains that the magic 'e' makes the vowel say its name. Repeat this activity with other cvc words.

- Play 'It's Magic!' Make a set of cvc word cards (they must make a word when magic 'e' is added). Make a set of magic 'e' cards – sprinkle glitter around the 'e' to make it look magical. Make a corresponding set of word cards such as 'mate', 'hate', 'cane' etc. Give each child a card and when you (as Marvo) wave your magic wand they should congregate into the correct sets of three. For example, three children who each have the cards 'mat', 'magic e', and 'mate' should stand together.

## Focus of Learning

Looking at the role and effect of 'magic e'

20

## Practical Activities

- Play 'Marvo's Magic Hat'. Make a set of top hat-shaped bingo boards with cvc words written on. Make a set of magic 'e' letter cards and a set of wand cards the same size and shape. Put these cards in the middle of the table in a top hat. Give each child a board and pen. The children take turns to pick a card out of Marvo's hat. If they pick a magic 'e' card they turn one of their cvc words into an new word. If they pick a wand card they rub out all of their magic 'e's!

- Play 'Make it Match'. Make a set of cards to play a simple pairs game, for example, write 'pip' on one card and 'pipe' on another. To make it more interesting write some cvc words on top hat-shaped cards and corresponding words on wand-shaped cards.

- Play 'Spin the Magic'. Give each child a headband to wear. Make a selection of cvc word cards and place them in a top hat in the middle of the table. Place one cvc word card on each child's headband. Make a spinner with three magic 'e's, a picture of a wand and a picture of a top hat. The children take turns to spin the spinner. If it lands on magic 'e' the child selects a cvc word that another child in the group has on his or her headband, and must be able to say which word he or she has made. If they are correct they keep the card and the child whose card has been taken chooses another card from the top hat. If the spinner lands on the magic wand the child is able to take everyone's card and say the correct words. If it lands on a top hat he or she must put all their cards back in the top hat. The winner is the child who collects the most cards.

## Cross-curricular Links

- **DESIGN & TECHNOLOGY** – Design and make a top hat to wear.

- **ICT** – Turn a programmable robot into 'Marvo'. Ask the children to programme the robot to follow a route and collect magic 'e' words.

- **DRAMA / ROLE PLAY** – Create a magic show. For example, it could be linked to Literacy by focusing on initial blends or vowels.

## Art and Display

- Make a top hat and wand. Display this with cvc words that can be changed using magic 'e'.

- Make a poster advertising Marvo's Marvellous Magic.

21

# Apples and Bananas

## Whole-class Starter

- Sing *Apples and Bananas (The Vowel Song)* (see page 72 for the words). Ask the children to explain what happens to some letters in the song. Explain that the letters that change are called 'vowels' and they are 'a', 'e', 'i', 'o' and 'u'.

- Play 'Pass the Bag Around the Ring'. The children sit in a circle and when a bag full of letters, which includes a lot of vowels, is passed around they all sing, "Pass the bag around the ring, round the ring, round the ring; Pass the bag around the ring, stop right here!" (to the tune of 'London Bridge is Falling Down'). Whoever has the bag when the song ends picks out a letter and the children sing "What letter have you got, have you got, have you got? What letter have you got, tell us now!" The child replies (singing), "I have got the vowel 'a' …" or "I have got the vowel 'e' …" or "I have not got a vowel … as you see". Carry on around the circle.

- Play 'Jump to the Vowel'. The children sit in a circle and say the alphabet in turn around the circle. When a child comes to a vowel he or she must jump up. Play again and start at a different child.

## Focus of Learning

Learning which letters are vowels

## Practical Activities

- Play 'Circle the Vowel'. Give each child in the group a whiteboard and pen. Place a wide selection of current words such as days of the week, months of the year, children's names etc. in a basket in the middle of the table. Children take a card, write the word on their whiteboard and circle the vowels. Repeat.

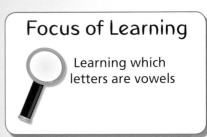

- Play 'It's a Question of Vowels'. Make a set of large question mark game boards (A3 size, see picture). The children work in pairs, each with a set of vowels and a 1–6 dice. They take turns to roll the dice and move a counter along the board. If they land on a picture of a cat they place the 'a' on the board. The object of the game is to get rid of all of their vowels first.

- Play 'Vowel Search'. Make a set of laminated wordsearch boards to include at least five of each vowel. The children colour in or circle the vowels. This could be a timed activity.

- Play 'Vowel Countdown'. Make a number of vowel cards in one colour and a number of consonant cards in a different colour. Place the cards face down in the middle of the table. Each child picks two vowel cards and five consonants and tries to make a word within a given time.

## Art and Display

- Paint or use collage materials to make giant apples and bananas for display using *The Vowel Song*.

- Cut out apple shapes and banana shapes in shades of red, green and yellow, papers or fabrics and make a collage.

- Make a clay tile. Cut out an apple and a banana shape and attach to the tiles. Paint when dry.

## Cross-curricular Links

- **GEOGRAPHY** – Draw a map of the journey of a banana. Plot on a world map where apples and bananas come from.

- **MUSIC** – Use percussion to accompany the song.

- **SCIENCE** – Find out which vitamins and minerals are in apples and bananas. Make a healthy eating poster.

# Pass the Jam Jim

## Focus of Learning

Looking at cvc words (consonant, vowel, consonant)

## Whole-class Starter

- Read and enjoy *Pass the Jam Jim* written by Kaye Umansky, illustrated by Margaret Chamberlain (Red Fox). Look at the words 'Jam' and 'Jim' from the title and ask the children questions such as "How many letters?", "How many vowels?", "How many consonants?" Explain to the children that the words 'jam' and 'Jim' are cvc words because they are made up of consonant, vowel, consonant.

- Place a selection of individual letters on the board. Ask the children to take turns to come out and make a cvc word such as 'cat', 'pot', 'hen', 'pig', 'run'.

- Play 'Jump on the Jam Jim Jam'. Read the story again (slowly), emphasising the cvc words. When the children hear a cvc word they stand up.

## Practical Activities

- Play 'CVC Three'. Make a large board covered with individual letters – enough to make lots of cvc words! Give each child three cubes and a whiteboard. In pairs the children take turns to find a cvc word by placing their three cubes on the letters on the board. If a correct cvc word is made the child writes the word on his or her whiteboard.

- Make jam pot-shaped zig-zag books. Ask the children to write their own 'Jam Jim' story using as many cvc words as possible. For example:

  'Jim put the jam in the pot and it was hot.

  Dot got the lot.

  "Oh it's hot!" said Dot.

  Mum got the pot and put it by the cat …' and so on.

- Play 'Pick a Pot'. Collect a number of small pots. In each pot place three letters to make a cvc word. Make a set of laminated boards with six cvc pictures on each board (every board must be different). The pictures on the boards must correspond to the words in the pots. Each child takes a turn to pick a pot and make the cvc word. If the cvc word corresponds to one of their pictures the child places the pot and letters on the appropriate picture.

## Art and Display

- Create a large pot of jam (for display with cvc words) either using paint or collage materials.

- Design labels for jam pots using watercolour pencils.

- Use chalk pastels or paint to draw giant strawberries and add these to the display.

## Cross-curricular Links

- **SCIENCE** – Taste different jams and identify the fruits. Draw a picture to show the story 'From fruit to jam'.

- **DESIGN & TECHNOLOGY** – Make a variety of food items using jam and take the children on a 'jammy picnic'.

- **MATHS** – Weigh different fruits or sugar. For capacity, compare different-sized jam jars and use a variety of objects to find their capacity.

- **MUSIC** – Make up a 'Jam Jim Jam' rap. Ask the children to get into groups of three. Each child should select an instrument or use body percussion to create their own rap using the words 'Jam Jim Jam'!

# The Tiny Seed

## Whole-class Starter

- After reading *The Tiny Seed* by Eric Carle (Puffin Books) show the children a tiny seed and ask them to close their eyes and listen for the middle phoneme – 'ee'.

- Ask the children to think of other double 'ee' words. Write them on the board. Explain to the children that the double 'ee' is only one phoneme – two letters, one phoneme. Demonstrate this by adding 'sound buttons' under a double ee word such as: <u>s</u> <u>ee</u> <u>d.</u>

- Play 'Phoneme Friends'. Each child quickly chooses the nearest person to them as their phoneme friend. The teacher picks a word off the board and the children decide with their friend how many phonemes the word has. The children use their fingers to count the phonemes and when the teacher says "Phoneme fingers!" the children hold up their fingers and the teacher can quickly see who is correct.

## Practical Activities

- Play 'A Seed in Need'. Make a set of large flowers with lots of petals. Set the minute timer and ask the children to write double 'ee' words on each petal. To make this game more difficult reduce the time given.

- Play 'Feed the Seed'. For this game you will need a set of cut-out flowerpots, soil, a seed, a flower stem, watering can, flower head, six petals and two leaves (laminate all these pieces). The object of the game is to make the flower picture. For a small group, place a selection of letters in the middle of the table. Ask the children to make a double 'ee' word such as 'seed', 'feed', 'weed' etc. The first child to make the word starts building his or her flower picture by placing the flowerpot in the correct place on the board.

- The children could write their own version of *The Tiny Seed* in a decorated book.

## Art and Display

- Make a large flower in the style of Eric Carle's *The Tiny Seed* by tearing tissue paper into large petal shapes and overprinting in shades of brown, yellow and orange. Display with a collection of 'ee' words.

- Make 3D bees using papier mâché on inflated balloons. When dry, cut the balloons in half and use this as a base for the bee's body. Paint yellow and black stripes on the body using thick poster paint. Add antennae (pipe cleaners) and wings made out of wire and tissue paper. Use pipe cleaners for legs and add a small cone-shaped piece of card for the sting! Add these to the display.

- Make individual flowerpot pictures using coloured paper.

- Make a large flowerpot for display. Children cut out flower shapes and leaves from coloured paper and stick randomly around the pot to create a stunning plant in a pot picture! Add 3D papier mâché bees. Write the correct 'ee' word under each bee.

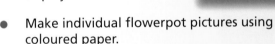

## Cross-curricular Links

- **DESIGN & TECHNOLOGY** – Design and make a seed packet.

- **SCIENCE** – Investigate the statement 'A plant needs water in order to grow'.

- **ICT** – Use a paint package to draw and label the parts of a flower.

- **GEOGRAPHY** – Draw an imaginary map of a seed's journey.

# Consonant Cauldron

## Whole-class Starter

- Winnie the Witch (you in role) visits the class. She has tried to make words but only has vowels. She puts a selection of vowels on the board and tries to make a word. Then she asks the children for help. They tell her that she needs more letters and give her an example. Winnie exclaims loudly, "I need my consonant cauldron!" She produces her cauldron (which secretly has consonants placed inside) … Winnie explains that she only needs five vowels ('a', 'e', 'i', 'o', 'u'); the other vowels she will turn into 'consonants'. Winnie throws the vowels into the cauldron saying, "Hubble, bubble, vowel in trouble, make me a consonant at the double!" Out of the cauldron she produces lots of consonants.

## Focus of Learning

Learning about consonants and vowels

- Play 'I Am a Consonant'. Make a set of alphabet cards, one for each child. Give out the cards and, on a signal, ask the children to sort themselves into vowels and consonants. The children swap all the cards and repeat the activity.

## Practical Activities

- Play 'Consonant Cauldron'. Give each child a laminated cauldron card. Place a selection of letters – vowels and consonants – in a cauldron in the middle of the table. Each child takes a turn to pick a letter. If it is a consonant they place it on their cauldron but if it is a vowel they put it back into the cauldron.

- Play 'Consonant Cones'. Using a selection of cones, attach a letter to each cone. Spread the cones out over a large area. Give each child a small hoop. The object of the game is to throw a hoop over a consonant cone.

- Play 'Musical Consonants'. Place a letter under each chair so it is not visible. When the music plays the children walk around the chairs, and when the music stops they sit on a chair and look underneath to see what letter they have. If it is a consonant they remain in the game. If it is a vowel they are out!

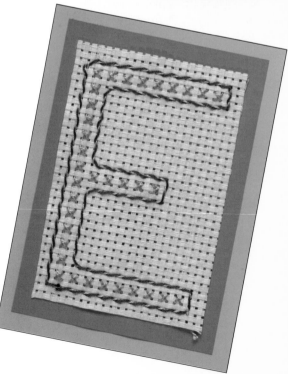

### Art and Display

- Make a witch and a cauldron and display with letters that are consonants.

- Make a Victorian sampler or sew a consonant or vowel on to binca.

- Print with consonant-shaped sponges.

### Cross-curricular Links

- **SCIENCE** – Investigate what happens when different substances are mixed. For example, oil and water, sugar and water.

- **PSHE** – Warm up circle time with 'Consonant Mix Up!' With the children in a circle, tell them which letter of the alphabet they are. When you say, "Consonant!" all the consonants change places; when you say, "Vowel!" all the vowels change places, and when you say, "Alphabet!" they all change places!

# Grammar

# Slowly the Snail

## Whole-class Starter

- Collect some snails. Together, look carefully at how they move. Ask the children to describe the movement of the snail. Write the words on the board. Ask the children what they notice about these words (they all end in 'ly'). Explain that these words are 'adverbs' and that they describe the snail's movement. Return the snails to the wild afterwards.

- Read 'The Snail' by Jean Kenward (published in *Scholastic Themes for Early Years*, Scholastic). Using the letters of the word 'snail' ask the children to help make a class acrostic poem.

## Focus of Learning

Learning about adverbs

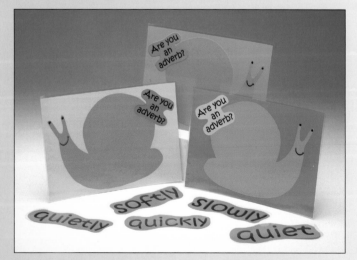

## Practical Activities

- Play 'Are You an Adverb?' Make a set of large, laminated, colourful snails. Also make a selection of word cards, some that are adverbs and some that are not. Place the cards in a basket and ask each child to pick out a word card. If it is an adverb the child writes it on his or her snail. If it is not an adverb he or she puts it back in the basket.

- Using the adverbs collected, ask the children to work in small groups to write creatively on large snail-shaped paper. Encourage them to start each sentence with an adverb.

30

- Using the ideas from the above group activity, prompt each child to write their own super snail sentences on small snail-shaped paper.

- Play 'Snail Trail'. Make a set of large snails each with a word written on, for example, 'slow', 'gentle', 'soft', 'quiet', 'quick', 'careful' etc. Place the cards in the hall or outside area to make a trail, and connect the snails by using silver thread or paper. In small groups the children follow the snail trail, stopping at each snail to change the word to an adverb by writing it on their whiteboard.

## Art and Display

- Sponge print or paint a large snail using shades of brown and yellow. When dry, varnish with PVA glue to give a shiny effect. Add silver paper for the trail, and display with adverbs and the children's writing.

- Look carefully at a snail shell and use pastels or watercolours to copy the pattern.

- Use quilling technique to make a snail picture.

## Cross-curricular Links

- **MUSIC** – Give each child an instrument and, using the adverb cards, ask them to pick a card and play their instrument in the style of the adverb picked.

- **SCIENCE** – Make a small fact file about the life of a snail. Ask the children to investigate habitat, food, predators, movement etc.

- **ICT** – Turn a programmable robot into a snail and give it instructions to follow a trail.

# Pants

## Whole-class Starter

- Read and enjoy *Pants* written by Giles Andreae, illustrated by Nick Sharratt (Picture Corgi). Talk about the different pants in the book and ask the children to think of more wacky pants! Explain that the words in the book that describe the pants are called 'adjectives' – describing words.

## Focus of Learning

Learning about adjectives

- Play 'Pants with a Partner'. Make a set of colourful, patterned pants – different from the ones in the book. Give each pair of children a whiteboard and pen and ask them to think of adjectives to describe each pair of pants.

- Think of ideas for a new book called 'Socks'. The children could work in small groups to write adjectives on large, sock-shaped paper. Share ideas and work as a class to write a book about socks.

## Practical Activities

- Write pants poems using as many adjectives as possible.

- Play 'Pinch the Pants'. Make or buy an enormous pair of pants! Use double-sided tape to stick lots of pictures of pants onto the large pair. One child is chosen to wear the pants and a blindfold, and to stand in the middle of the circle. The other children are given some adjective cards which describe a pair of pants. On a given signal the children creep slowly towards the centre of the circle and try to pinch the correct pair of pants without being touched by the child wearing the blindfold. The object of the game is to collect all of the pairs of pants that match the adjectives on the cards. If a child is touched he or she is out of the game.

- Play 'I Spy an Adjective'. Put a selection of Nick Sharratt books on a table. Give each child a magnifying glass and ask them to find as many adjectives as they can. These could be written on a whiteboard, in a book or on a large piece of paper.

## Art and Display

- Paint and collage large pairs of patterned pants for display. Add adjectives and the children's poems.

- Draw and create new pants patterns and add these to the display.

- Buy a large pair of plain pants. Ask each child to cut out a shape from fabric and sew it on to make a whole-class pair of crazy pants.

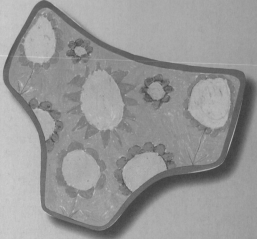

## Cross-curricular Links

- **FUN!** – Have a Crazy Pants Day! Wear your pants over normal school clothes!

- **DESIGN & TECHNOLOGY** – Make pants-shaped biscuits and ask the children to decorate them.

33

# Vigorous Verbs

## Focus of Learning

Learning about verbs

## Whole-class Starter

- Play 'Vigorous Verbs'. Create work stations in the hall or outside area. Put a sign by each station such as 'jump', 'hop', 'skip', 'walk', 'bounce', 'run' etc. Read the words to the children and then send small groups to each station. Give each group one minute to do each activity (take photos of each activity). Bring the children together and ask them to explain what they have been doing. Explain that the words on the cards are called 'verbs' and these are 'doing' words. Ask the children to think of other verbs. Make a collection of 'doing' words.

- Put a selection of action pictures on the board and ask the children to use a verb to describe each action, for example, 'kick', 'jump', 'run', 'dive', 'climb' etc.

- Play 'Is it a Verb?' Make two sets of cards, one set with verbs written on, and one set that are not verbs but are words that children can read. Put the words in a bag. With the children in a circle, pass the bag around the circle to music. When the music stops a child picks out a card. If it is a verb he or she does that action; if it is not a verb he or she passes the bag on.

## Practical Activities

- Play 'Find it, Write it, Do it!' Prepare lots of simple sentence cards which have a very obvious verb. For example, 'The green frog hopped out of the water', 'The little mouse ran into his hole'. Place these cards around the room or school. Give each child a whiteboard and pen. They should visit each card, find the verb, write it on the whiteboard and do the action.

- Play 'Make it Make Sense'. Place a selection of verb cards in the middle of the table. The children take turns to pick a card and with a partner discuss how to put the verb into a sentence that makes sense. Write the sentence on a whiteboard and discuss the sentence with the rest of the group.

- Play 'Search for a Verb'. Make a giant wordsearch – this could be chalked on the playground. Include lots of verbs in the squares of the wordsearch. Give each child about five beanbags. The object of the game is to throw the beanbags and hit a verb. If a verb is hit, hoot a hooter and ask the child to put the verb into a sentence.

## Art and Display

- Paint or collage large action characters and use these to create a 'Vigorous Verbs' display. Include the children's action photos from the whole-class starter.

- Design a 'Vigorous Verbs' poster.

## Cross-curricular Links

- **ICT** – Design and make a 'Vigorous Verbs' book.
- **P.E.** – Create a circuit-training course using the actions you have collected during the vigorous verbs activities.

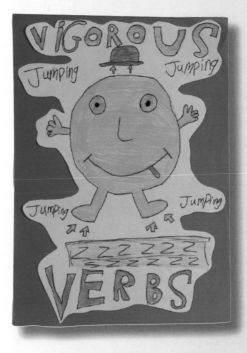
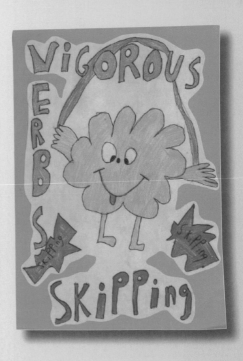

# Know Your Nouns

## Whole-class Starter

- Watch and enjoy a story such as *William's Wish Wellingtons* (BBC Children's Video, 20th Century Fox). Talk about William's Wellingtons – ask the children what they wear on rainy days. Dress a child in wet-weather clothes such as a raincoat, wellingtons, rain hat, umbrella etc. Label each item of clothing and tell the children that these words are called 'nouns', specifically 'common nouns'. Tell the children that a noun is a 'thing'.

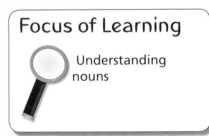

### Focus of Learning

Understanding nouns

- Play 'Wishing Wellies'. With the children in a circle, place a pair of wellingtons in the middle – the 'Wishing Wellies'. A child turns to put the wellies on and say the rhyme, "Wishing wellies, wishing wellies, I would like to go over the hills, beyond the sea to a place that I don't know". The child then names a country or city and a reason for going. Write the place on the board and explain that these are nouns too, 'proper nouns', and all begin with a capital letter.

- Play 'Know your Nouns'. Make a set of common noun cards and a set of proper noun cards. Give each child a card. Place two hoops on the carpet, one labelled 'Proper nouns' and the other labelled 'Common nouns'. Play some gentle music and ask the children to place their card in the correct hoop.

## Practical Activities

- Play 'It's a noun'. For this game you will need to have a world map and other objects accessible. Label a spinner with the words 'Common noun' and 'Proper noun'. Each child takes a turn to spin the spinner. If it lands on 'Common noun' each child in the group writes the common noun on a label and places it on the correct object. If it lands on 'Proper noun' each child in the group writes the proper noun on a label and puts it on the place on the world map.

- Take the children on a noun hunt – using both inside and outside space. Make each child a 'Noun Collector's Book' and as they walk around they write the nouns in their books. Alternatively, the children could look for examples of nouns in books.

- Make a noun alphabet zig-zag book using common and proper nouns on alternate pages. For example: 'apple', 'Bernard', 'cat', 'Denmark', 'elephant', 'France' and so on.

## Art and Display

- Use paint and collage materials to create pictures for a display about nouns.

- The children could draw their names in large letters. On each letter draw pictures of a noun. For example, for the name 'Liz' draw ladybirds or ladders on the 'L', insects or India on the 'i', and 'zebras' on the 'z'. Add these to the display.

- Make a noun collage using words and pictures cut out of newsprint or magazines.

## Cross-curricular Links

- **GEOGRAPHY** – Pick a country and find common nouns and proper nouns associated with that country. For example, for France – 'croissant', 'baguette', 'Eiffel Tower', 'Mona Lisa'.

- **HISTORY** – What's in a name? Ask each child to find out where his or her name comes from and what it means.

- **MUSIC** – Create a noun rap.

# Pot of Plurals

## Whole-class Starter

- Show the children a selection of vegetables such as carrots, peas, beans, onions, potatoes etc. Ask the children to listen carefully. Hold up one carrot and say the word 'carrot'. Then hold up several carrots and say 'carrots'. Ask the children what they notice. Introduce the word 'plural' and explain that it means 'more than one'. Explain to the children that if there is only one of an object it is 'singular'.

- Play 'Perhaps it's a Plural'. On the carpet place a selection of pictures of singular and plural vegetables. Write the words 'singular' and 'plural' on the board. With the children in a circle, spin a bottle. Whoever it points to picks a card and places it in the correct column on the board. The child then writes the correct word underneath.

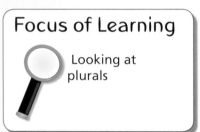

### Focus of Learning

Looking at plurals

## Practical Activities

- Play 'Plant a Plural'. Make a set of large, laminated beanstalk boards (with at least ten large leaves). Make a set of singular vegetable cards to place in the middle of the table. Give each child a beanstalk board and a pen. Each child takes a turn to pick a vegetable card and place it on a beanstalk leaf. When a child has two or more of the same vegetable they write the plural on the beanstalk pot and say, "I've planted a plural". The object of the game is to cover all the beanstalk leaves and collect as many plurals as possible.

- Play 'Plastered with Plurals'. Make a large set of singular and plural vegetable word cards. The children should form four teams ('peas', 'carrots', 'beans', 'sprouts'), with one child wearing a picture of the team vegetable and standing in a hoop. Place the vegetable word cards randomly all over the wall. The children line up in teams and, on a given signal, the first person in each team runs to the wall, finds the plural of his or her team's vegetable, takes it back to the team who pass the word to the next team member going over heads and under legs alternately. Finally, the child at the back runs to the child in the hoop and 'plasters' the plural on to the child. Repeat for a one minute and the winning team is the one who has plastered the most plurals on to their team member.

## Art and Display

- Make a giant 3D pot and display this with a variety of giant, painted vegetables and labels, including plurals.

- The children could draw and colour vegetable shapes to make their name.

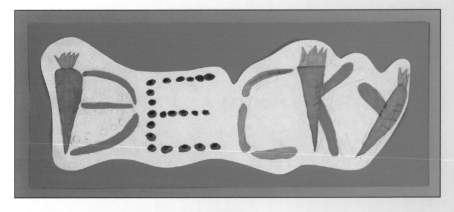

- Bring in a variety of vegetables and demonstrate how to do close, observational drawings in pencil.

- Print with vegetable colours on vegetable shaped paper, or use collage materials to make a vegetable.

- Make vegetables from papier mâché and paint. They could be giant-sized!

## Cross-curricular Links

- **DESIGN & TECHNOLOGY** – Design and make a large packet to carry some vegetables home from the market.

- **ROLE PLAY** – Make a vegetable market stall.

- **SCIENCE** – Plant and grow a variety of vegetables.

# Crazy Contractions

## Whole-class Starter

- Read and enjoy the book *Don't Do That* by Tony Ross (Red Fox). Read the book again and every time there is a contraction replace it with the two words. For example, 'would not', 'could not', 'is not', etc. Discuss these changes and explain contractions to the children.

- Play 'Collect your Contraction'. Make a set of phrase cards and a set of corresponding contraction cards. Give each child a card and, on a given signal, ask the children to find their partners.

- Play 'Create a Contraction'. Give each child a whiteboard and a pen. Place a selection of letters and apostrophes randomly on the board – the letters must make a contraction. Ask the children to create a contraction.

## Practical Activities

- Make a multicoloured book for each child. The title on the front could be *When the 'o' has gone*! The children write a phrase such as 'do not', 'could not', 'would not', on each page and fold the page so that the 'o' is hidden. Then add the apostrophe on each page (see picture).

- Play 'Contraction Collectors'. Give each child a special badge, a magnifying glass and a selection of suitable texts. Ask them to collect as many examples of contractions that they can. The children could write them in a little book called 'My Contraction Collection'. This activity lends itself to a walk around the school environment, collecting contractions.

## Art and Display

- Talk about the face on the front of *Don't Do That*. Look at the proportions and compare them to the children's faces. Ask the children to draw portraits of each other.

- Make a large picture of Nellie and add contractions to the display. Create smaller angels by printing a hand and adding a painted head and wings.

- Make clay faces.

- Look at faces in art such as Paul Klee, Arcimboldo, Picasso. Make pictures in the same style using a variety of media.

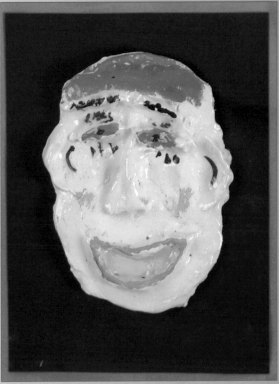

- Sculpt faces using newspaper, modroc and a cardboard tube.

## Cross-curricular Links

- **PSHE** – Discuss times when the children have been told 'don't do that'.

- **SCIENCE** – Investigate the relationship between smelling and tasting.

# Roaming Romans

## Whole-class Starter

- As part of a Roman topic, discuss with the children the characteristics of a Roman soldier, for example, 'brave', 'strong', 'courageous'. Make a list on one side of the board. Then ask the children to think about something else that is brave, strong, and courageous and write their suggestions down the other side of the board. Can the children put the two things together to make a sentence? For example, 'A Roman soldier is as strong as an ox', 'A Roman soldier is as courageous as a lion' etc. Explain to the children that sentences like these are called 'similes'.

### Focus of Learning

Looking at similes

- Play 'Sort the Similes'. Make two sets of cards, one set with phrases such as 'as brave as a ...', 'as fearless as a ...' etc, and the other set with words such as 'knight', 'lion', 'mouse', 'my teacher' etc. Give each child a card and, on a given signal, prompt the children to form pairs to make a simile. Repeat this activity several times. This activity could be played as 'Silly Similes'.

## Practical Activities

- Write about and draw a Roman soldier, describing his uniform using similes.

- In small groups the children dress up as different Roman characters and describe themselves in terms of similes. For example, an Emperor could be 'as wise as an owl', a gladiator could be 'as fearless as a lion', a slave could be 'as timid as a mouse'.

- Play 'Secret Similes'. In a small group one child sits in front of the other children wearing a headband. Place a word card on the headband so that he/she is unable to see the word. The other children take turns to describe the word using a simile. For example, the word on the label could be 'bear'. The children could say, 'brave like a lion', 'brown like a chocolate', 'fierce like a Roman soldier', 'loud like thunder' etc. The child wearing the label has to guess what word is written.

- Play 'Simple Similes'. Make a set of Bingo Boards with a variety of different pictures such as a fire engine, nurse, mouse etc. Make a set of simile cards which describe the pictures such as 'as red as an apple', 'as kind as my friend', 'as quiet as a whisper'. Each child takes a turn to pick a card and decide which picture it most relates to.

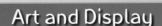

- Make a mosaic animal, using squares of coloured paper.

- Sculpt a Roman soldier using wire, newspaper and modroc. Spray or paint black. Display with a sign asking the children to guess the actions of the Roman soldier.

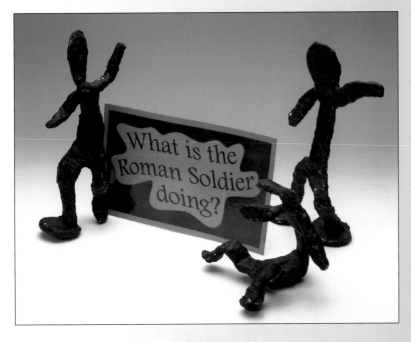

## Art and Display

- Use collage to create large Roman soldiers for a display about similes. Include the children's writing and drawings of Roman soldiers.

- Paint individual Roman soldiers and add to the display.

## Cross-curricular Links

- **DRAMA** – Have a Roman feast, battle or day.

- **DESIGN & TECHNOLOGY** – Design and make either a Roman shield or helmet.

- **ICT** – Use a Word program to word process a simile poem. Ask the children to import their own border or picture. Encourage them to use a Roman style font.

# What About Water?

## Whole-class Starter

- The Queen of Questions (you in role) arrives in the classroom, wearing an outfit covered with question words such as 'What?', 'Where?', 'When?', 'Why?', 'How?' and pictures of wellies and an umbrella. Ask questions such as "Why does it have to rain?", "Where does the rain come from?", "How does the rain get into the clouds?", "What is water?", "When will it stop?" Explain that you are the Queen of Questions and produce a very large question mark. Talk about the words on the outfit. Discuss question marks with the children.

- Play 'What's the Question?' Write statements on the board such as 'It is a liquid', 'Rain falls from the clouds', 'It turns to snow'. The children work in pairs to think of questions to those answers such as 'What is water?', 'Where does rain come from?'

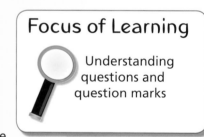

### Focus of Learning

Understanding questions and question marks

## Practical Activities

- Make a question-and-answer booklet or fact file about water and rain on droplet-shaped paper.

- Play 'Complete the question'. Make a set of laminated question cards with the first word missing, for example, '_____ is water?', '_____ does water come from?' Write question words on a spinner. The children take turns to spin the spinner, decide which question card best fits the question word spun and write it on their question card.

- Play 'Quest for a Question'. Give each child a magnifying glass, a non-fiction book about water – the same book for each child – and a large laminated question mark covered with question words. Put numbers in a bag which correspond to page numbers in the book. Pick out a number, show it to the children who should quickly turn to that page and find an example of a question word. Then the children cover the correct word on their question mark with a counter. The object of the game is to cover all of the question words.

## Art and Display

- Paint a large person in rainwear and display them, surrounded by questions about water.

- Use a marbling technique to create backgrounds for other work, or cut out raindrop shapes to use as a collage and add these to the display.

- Weave with different blues to decorate the front of a topic book on water.

## Cross-curricular Links

- **SCIENCE** – Investigate the following questions: 'What is steam?', 'What is evaporation?', 'What is ice?', 'What is a cloud?'

- **GEOGRAPHY** – Find out about 'The river's journey'. Go on a river boat trip.

- **DANCE** – Create a dance based on 'The river's journey'. Begin with the tiny spring bubbling out of the earth, the quick flowing of the stream, the meandering river and the pounding sea!

- **PSHE** – Discuss drought countries and the effect of not having enough water. Talk about the benefits of drinking lots of water. Discuss the uses of water.

# Suddenly!

- Read and enjoy the book *Suddenly!* by Colin McNaughton (Anderson Press). Read the story again but without using any expression. Ask the children what they noticed about the way the story was read. Which did they prefer and why? Discuss the use of bold type and the effect it has on the way words are read. Ask the children if they know the symbol at the end of the word 'suddenly' (an exclamation mark). Discuss the use of the exclamation mark.

- Give each child a whiteboard and a pen. Reread the story but this time explain to the children that they are going to look at the actions of the wolf and write a word with an exclamation mark. For example, 'Thud!', 'Bang!, 'Ouch!' etc. Make a list of words on the board. Discuss with the children the types of words that they have used.

## Focus of Learning

Understanding and using exclamation marks

## Practical Activities

- Play 'Let's Explain It'. Make a set of large wolf faces, and on the back, write one word from the story, for example, 'bang', 'thud', 'shopping', 'Preston'. Give each child in the group an exclamation mark and a pig mask to wear. The children work together to look at a wolf picture and decide if it needs an exclamation mark. If it does, they stick one on; if it does not they move to the next picture.

- Play 'Exclamation Detectives'. Give each child a detective badge, a magnifying glass and a selection of books. Ask the detectives to find as many exclamation marks as possible before you (as the wolf) shout "Suddenly!"

- Play 'What's the Word, Mr Wolf?' Make lots of large word cards such as 'thud', 'suddenly', 'bang', 'telephone', 'shopping', 'chair' etc. One child wears a wolf mask and holds the cards with his/her back to the other children; they each stand in a hoop of their own. Place large exclamation marks around the hall or large area. The children stand in their hoops and chant, "What's the word, Mr Wolf?" Mr Wolf turns around and shows and says a word. If it does not need an exclamation mark the children take one step forward towards Mr Wolf. If it does need an exclamation mark the children run to collect an exclamation mark and return to their hoop before the wolf catches them!

## Art and Display

- Create pictures of Preston and a silhouette of the wolf using pastels.

- Draw and use watercolours to make a picture of Preston in a new pair of dungarees and add it to the display with a speech bubble containing an exclamation mark.

- Create a display with a large picture of Preston, the wolf and words that use exclamation marks.

- Make little pig money boxes using papier mâché and paint.

## Cross-curricular Links

- **PSHE** – Discuss the actions of the wolf and talk about dangerous situations, for example climbing on bins and roofs.

- **ICT** – In small groups, make a PowerPoint presentation using words, pictures and exclamation marks.

- **DESIGN & TECHNOLOGY** – Use construction materials to make a new shopping trolley for Preston.

- **GEOGRAPHY** – Make an imaginary map of Preston's journey.

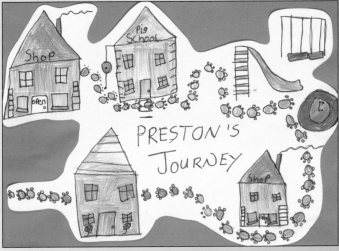

# Not Now, Bernard

## Whole-class Starter

- Read *Not Now, Bernard* by Tony Ross (Red Fox) and use exaggerated voices to emphasise each character's speech.

- Make a set of large characters from the story and some large speech bubbles. Place one of the characters on the board with a speech bubble, for example, Bernard with a speech bubble saying, "Hello Dad." Show the children how to write "Hello Dad" using speech marks. Repeat with other characters.

- Make a human sentence. Write each of the words and punctuation from the following sentence on separate cards: '"Not now, Bernard" said his mother.' Give each child a card and, on the words "Now, Bernard!", the children should order themselves to form the sentence correctly. Swap the cards and repeat.

## Focus of Learning

Understanding and using speech marks

## Practical Activities

- Play 'Simply Speech'. Give each child a laminated piece of text from the story and ask them to put in the speech marks.

- Play 'Mind the Monster' (a version of 'Stuck in the Mud'). One child, dressed as the monster, sits in a hoop with his/her eyes closed. Make a set of sentence cards from the story without the speech marks such as 'Hello Dad said Bernard.' Make another set such as 'The monster went upstairs.' Make lots of large laminated speech marks and place them around the monster. Pairs of children sit in hoops while you give each pair a sentence to complete. The children read their sentence and decide if it needs speech marks or not. If it does, the children creep to collect their speech marks without the monster hearing them. If the monster is disturbed he chases the children away and they put the speech marks back. The winners are those who have completed the most sentences. Sentences could be stuck to the wall when complete.

- Play 'Spot the Speech Marks'. Either give the children a selection of books and ask them to find the speech marks, or prepare a variety of laminated texts and ask the children to stick a spot on the speech marks.

## Art and Display

- Paint or collage a giant monster and Bernard. Add speech bubbles and sentences using speech marks to the display.

- Choose a picture from the story and draw and colour using watercolour pencils. Ask the children to add a sentence with speech marks.

## Cross-curricular Links

- **LITERACY** – Write a blurb for the story.

- **PSHE** – Discuss the issues of feelings or parental roles.

- **GEOGRAPHY** – Draw a bird's-eye view of Bernard's house. Use the rooms in the story to draw the plan.

- **DESIGN & TECHNOLOGY** – Design and paint a new T-shirt for Bernard or design and make a new toy for Bernard, such as a rocket, using a wide variety of materials.

# Handa's Hen

## Whole-class Starter

- Read the story of *Handa's Hen* by Eileen Browne (Walker Books). Discuss the apostrophe in the title. Ask the children a series of questions such as, "How many Handas are in the story?", "How many hens are in the story?", "Why is there an 's' at the end of Handa's name if there is only one Handa?" Show the children a giant apostrophe and explain its function. Ask them if they can find the apostrophe in the title and explain that it means 'the hen belonging to Handa'.

- Make giant words from the story such as 'Handa', 'hen', 'eggs', 'Grandma', 'friend', 'breakfast', 'bowl' etc. Make a giant apostrophe 's'. Ask the children to take turns to make a phrase using the apostrophe 's' and the giant words, for example, 'Handa's hen', 'Handa's friend' etc.

## Practical Activities

- Play 'Apostrophe Agents'. Make each child a badge saying 'Apostrophe Agent'. Give them each a magnifying glass and a selection of books. Challenge the agents to find as many apostrophe 's' as they can. Ask the children to write the words complete with apostrophes on a whiteboard or in their agent's diary.

- Help the children to write their own creative story based on the book, for example, 'Handa's Caterpillars', 'Handa's Tadpoles', 'Handa's Eggs'.

- Play 'Animated Apostrophes'. Collect a selection of props relating to the story, for example, a hen, eggs, a dress for Handa, a hat and slippers for Grandma etc. Make a selection of individual cards saying 'Handa's dress', 'Grandma's slippers', 'the hen's eggs' etc. With the children sitting in a circle, place the props in the centre. Give each child a card and, on a given signal, they read the card and quickly collect the correct props and return to their place. Each child must then explain who or what they are, for example, if a child's card says 'the hen's eggs' the child would collect a hen's mask and some pretend eggs. The child would then explain that the eggs belong to the hen.

## Art and Display

- Use paint and collage materials to make a large hen and a picture of Handa for display. Add phrases and words using apostrophes.

- Make pompom chicks using wool.

- Draw and use watercolours to paint the hen from the story. Add these to the display.

- Make camouflage pictures by painting and collaging a background and adding an animal to create a 3D effect.

## Cross-curricular Links

- **GEOGRAPHY** – Draw a story map showing Handa's journey to find the hen.

- **MUSIC** – Use percussion instruments to depict the animals, creatures and settings in the story.

- **DANCE** – Retell the story through dance. Use a motif to depict Handa's friendship. Allow the children to explore and create their own movements for each creature. Choose music suitable for each creature.

# Santa's Simple Sentences

## Whole-class Starter

- Mrs (or Father) Christmas (you in role) arrives in an agitated state! Santa has forgotten who he is and what he is supposed to do and he needs the children's help! Can they write some simple sentences so that he has a check list to remind him? Ask the children to write a list of anything to do with Santa, for example, 'red coat', 'white beard', 'black boots' and so on. Ask the children to put one of their ideas into a sentence. Talk about how to begin and end a sentence with capital letters and full stops.

## Focus of Learning

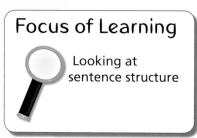

Looking at sentence structure

- Play 'Santa's Human Sentences'. Make word cards with which to make sentences about Santa (including a full stop), and attach them to a set of coloured bibs. Give individual children a bib to wear and, when they hear sleigh bells ring (use jingle bells), they make a simple sentence.

## Practical Activities

- Play 'Roll a Sentence'(you will need a set of skittles). Stick a word on each skittle and place the skittles randomly in a row. The children take turns to try and make a sentence by knocking down the skittles in the correct order.

- Play 'Ho! Ho! Ho!' Make sets of simple sentences chopped up into individual words. Place them in small sacks in the middle of the table. When Santa (you) says, "Ho! Ho! Ho!" each child takes a sack and sorts the sentence. The first child to sort the sentence shouts, "Ho! Ho! Ho!"

- Put a selection of pictures about Santa (for example, boots, beard, sack, toys etc) in the middle of the table. Each child picks a picture and writes a simple sentence about Santa on shaped paper.

- Play 'Spin and Spot'. Make a set of laminated bingo boards with six incorrect sentences. For example, 'santa has a red coat.' (the word 'santa' is all lower case), 'beard has Santa . a white' (a jumbled-up sentence). Make a spinner with the following labels: 'capital letter', 'full stop', 'jumbled', and a picture of Santa's face. The children take turns to spin the spinner and spot the mistake on their board by covering the mistake with a red spot. If the spinner lands on Santa, they clear their board. When all the children have spotted all the mistakes on their board they write the correct sentence under the incorrect ones.

- Play 'Santa Says'. Make a tape recording of several simple sentences about Santa (for example, 'Santa gives us presents', or 'I have a beard'). On a whiteboard the children write what they hear using capital letters and full stops.

## Art and Display

- Paint or use collage materials to make a giant Santa. Add a simple sentence about Santa to the display.

- Use 2D shapes and coloured paper to make a Santa and add this to the display.

- Make a Santa puppet.

- Use recycled materials to make a 3D Santa.

## Cross-curricular Links

- **DESIGN & TECHNOLOGY** – Make a Santa biscuit.

- **ICT** – Use a word-processing package to create mixed-up sentences. Ask the children to use their word-processing skills to correct the sentences.

# George and the Dragon

## Whole-class Starter

- Read and enjoy the story *George and the Dragon* by Chris Wormell (Red Fox), discussing character traits. At the back of the book have a pre-prepared very sad letter from the dragon, expressing his feeling of loneliness and his desire to return to his cave if the princess can be persuaded. He desperately needs some help. The letter is addressed to 'Whoever finds this letter'. Ask the children for ideas of how they can help the dragon. Write down and discuss their ideas.

## Focus of Learning

Understanding the use of persuasive language

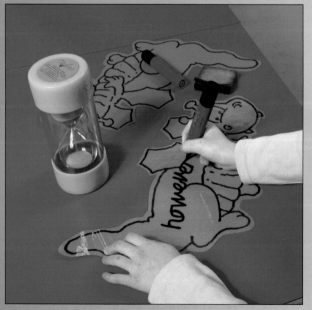

- Play 'Persuasive Pandemonium'. Make two sets of sentence cards: one set should contain persuasive sentences, such as 'Let me come back and I will use my fire to help you light all the stoves in the kingdom'; the other set with sentences that are not very persuasive, such as 'Let me come back and I will burn down your castle'. Label two hoops with the phrases 'persuasive sentence' and 'non-persuasive sentence'. Give each child a card and, on a given signal, they place their sentence in the appropriate hoop.

## Practical Activities

- Play 'A Time to Persuade'. Make a set of large, laminated dragon boards. Ask the children to work in pairs to beat the timer and write as many persuasive words as they can on their dragon boards.

- Ask the children to imagine they are the dragon and ask them to write a persuasive letter to the mouse, imploring the mouse to allow you back into the kingdom.

- Make a persuasive poster. On the poster the children must use their powers of persuasion to depict the dragon in a positive way. For example, the poster could say 'Although he is fierce he can protect us from our enemy' or 'His fire may be dangerous, however it will help us light our stoves'.

## Art and Display

- Use paint and collage materials to make a giant dragon and a small mouse. Add the children's persuasive sentences to the display, and smaller pictures of the dragon.

- Use a range of flame-coloured fabrics and sew on to hessian to create fire pictures.

- Make dragon silhouette pictures. Use strips of tissue in shades of red, yellow and orange to create a background. Cut out a dragon shape from black paper, and glue on to the background.

## Cross-curricular Links

- **R.E.** – Read and discuss the story of St George and the Dragon. Find out about the role of other saints, for example St Nicholas and St Francis of Assisi.

- **PSHE** – Discuss forgiveness and why it is important to forgive. Ask the children if they can think of a time when they have forgiven somebody.

- **DRAMA** – In small groups re-enact the story of George and the Dragon. The children could also re-enact the sequel: When the Dragon Returns.

# Lighthouse Keeper's Holiday

## Whole-class Starter

- Read *The Lighthouse Keeper's Lunch* by Ronda and David Armitage (Scholastic Hippo). Talk about where the stories are set, the main characters, and so on. Ask the children to talk with a partner for a few minutes about what makes a good story and what a good story needs – a setting, characters, plot, ending. Share their ideas as a class.

- Play 'Silly Stories'. Make a set of colour-coded cards, one for each aspect of a story. For example, six different story settings on red card, six different characters on blue card, six different plots on yellow card and six endings on green card (you will need to make a card for each child). Give each child a card and, on a given signal, they should form story groups – each group must have one card of each colour. The children then create an oral story out of the cards they have and share them with the rest of the class.

## Practical Activities

- Write a new lighthouse keeper adventure in a small book and illustrate.

- Play 'Roll a Story'. Make a large dice and on it write the words 'setting', 'character', 'plot', 'ending'. Place six very large pieces of paper around the room. The children take turns to roll the dice. If it lands on the word 'setting' the child writes a suitable sentence on one of the large pieces of paper. The next child rolls the dice and if it lands on 'setting' again that child writes another setting on another piece of paper. The object of the activity is to write a simple story in sequence.

- Play 'Story Search'. Place a selection of simple story books on the table. Give each child a piece of A3 paper divided into four sections with the words 'setting' in one section, 'characters' in another, 'plot' and 'ending'. Ask the children to look at a book and decide on the settings, characters etc. They write these on their A3 piece of paper.

- Play 'Select a Story'. With the children in a circle, one child chooses a story setting using the cards made earlier. They should place it in the middle of a circle. The next child chooses a character, the next a plot, and so on. Using these cards as prompts, create a whole-class, oral story.

## Art and Display

- Create wax resist lighthouses and display with a model lighthouse.

- Paint and collage a large lighthouse and character for display. Base the display on the children's new adventure for Mr Grinling and include words to help demonstrate story structure.

- Colour mix shades of blue for a background. Cut out seagull shapes from white paper and glue them onto the blue background.

## Cross-curricular Links

- **DESIGN & TECHNOLOGY** – Design a healthy lunch for Mr Grinling.

- **SCIENCE** – Investigate pulleys.

- **DRAMA** – Recreate the scenes from the story.

# Pizza

## Whole-class Starter

- In role as Pedro the Pizzamaker tell the children that you are going to show them how to make perfect pizzas. Demonstrate how to make a pizza and talk about the importance of doing things in the correct order. Explain that they must write the instructions so that they remember how to make the 'Perfect Pizza'. Demonstrate the type of words they will need to use, such as 'put', 'cut', 'make', 'sprinkle', 'grate', 'spread' and so on.

### Focus of Learning

Learning how to write instructions

- Play 'Pizza Partners'. Write a list of numbered instructions for making pizza on pizza-shaped paper or card. Jumble up the order. Working in pairs, give each pair a whiteboard and ask them to discuss with their pizza partner which instruction would come first. The children write the number on the whiteboard and hold it up for you, as Pedro, to check. Continue until all the instructions are in the correct order.

## Practical Activities

- Play 'Pieces of Pizza'. Make sets of laminated pizza pieces, each with an instruction written on (eight pieces for each child). Put the pizza pieces in a bag. The children take turns to pick a piece of pizza. If they pick the same piece twice it just goes back in the bag and the child misses a turn. When the children have each collected their eight pieces of pizza, say to them, "Make a perfect pizza!" and the children put their pieces in the correct order on a pizza-shaped board.

- Play 'Pedro's Pizza'. Make a set of large, laminated chef's hats. On each hat write eight simple instructions for making a pizza, but with the first word of each instruction missing. On a large spinner write the missing words such as 'cut', 'put', 'make', 'grate', 'knead', 'spread', 'add', 'sprinkle'. The children take turns to spin the spinner. Whatever word it lands on the child decides where to write it on their chef's hat.

- Write a pizza poem using an acrostic format. For example:

  Pizzas are my favourite food.
  In my tummy they are yummy!
  Zoos have pizza too, but
  Zebras don't eat pizza …
  At all!

## Art and Display

- Use collage materials to make a large pizza for display. Add the instructions for making the pizza.

- Make individual pizzas using collage materials and paint.

- Print a pizza. On round pieces of paper, sponge-print a red background. Use other items to print toppings, for example, corks for pepperoni, card edges for strips of ham or peppers, and so on.

- Use paint and collage materials to create a 'funny face' pizza.

## Cross-curricular Links

- **GEOGRAPHY** – Find out where pizza comes from and locate on a world map or globe.

- **DESIGN & TECHNOLOGY** – Use a variety of tools to create own pizzas. Then design and make a box to carry the pizza.

- **ROLE-PLAY** – Create a pizza parlour.

# Bonkers About Bikes

- Show the children *Bicycles* by Chris Oxlade (Heinemann First Library), a non-fiction book about bicycles. Discuss the features of a non-fiction text. Identify the contents page, index, glossary, headings etc. and discuss the function of each one.

- With the children in a circle, place a selection of fiction and non-fiction texts in the middle, plus two boxes labelled 'Fiction' and 'Non-fiction'. Each child takes a turn to pick up a book, put it in the correct box and give their reasons.

- Discuss what non-fiction books are used for (finding out information). Explain to the children that they are going to be bicycle detectives and they will need to listen carefully while you read out some facts about bikes. When the children have listened to you read aloud from the book, ask them to go to their tables and write one fact that they have heard and then return to the carpet with their fact. Each child shares his or her fact.

## Focus of Learning

Looking at non-fiction

## Practical Activities

- Help the children to make non-fiction, bicycle-shaped books in which to write facts about bicycles.

- Make a large bicycle timeline. Provide the children with pictures of bicycles. Ask them to use an information book to identify the bikes and place them in the correct order on the timeline.

- Play 'Beat the Bell'. Make a set of cards with non-fiction words such as 'contents', 'glossary' etc. Put these in a basket. Give each child a copy of a non-fiction book about bicycles. The children take turns to pick out a word and race to find the relevant place in the book. The first child to find it rings the bell.

- Make a set of large, laminated, non-fiction words and place these around the hall or open space, for example, 'Front cover', 'Back cover', 'Contents page', 'Title page', 'Index', 'Glossary'. Place features of non-fiction books in the middle of the floor, for example, title, author name, ISBN number, part of the contents page. On a given signal a child picks up one of these, identifies what it is and stands by the correct word. For example, if a child picks up 'Author name' he would stand by 'Front cover'. If he picks up the ISBN number he would stand by the words 'Back cover' and so on.

## Art and Display

- Sketch bicycles from long ago and parts of modern bicycles using charcoal. Display these with the children's writing about bikes.

- Make a clay tile and use various objects to imprint a bicycle shape.

- Create a giant bicycle using materials found around the school, for example, (clean!) dustbin lids for wheels, brooms for the bicycle frame etc.

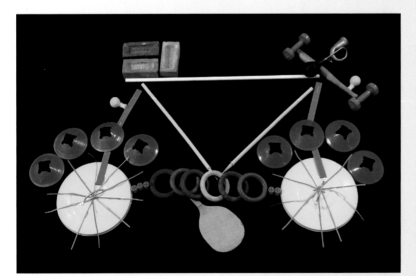

## Cross-curricular Links

- **ICT** – Use a paint package to draw a bicycle.

- **DANCE** – Use 'Bicycle Race' by Queen as a stimulus to create a group bicycle dance.

- **HISTORY** – Talk about bicycles in the past and how they have changed.

- **DESIGN & TECHNOLOGY** – Design and make a futuristic bicycle. Have fun!

# Monkey Do!

## Whole-class Starter

- Read and enjoy the story *Monkey Do!* by Allan Ahlberg and Andre Amstutz (Walker Books). Reread the story and ask the children to join in with the rhyming words. Talk about the words in the story that rhyme. Write them on the board.

## Focus of Learning

Looking at rhyme

- Play 'Monkey Do!' Make a set of rhyming cards using the same rhyming words as in the story, for example, 'chew', 'blue', 'run', 'bun', 'low', 'go', 'galore', 'score' and so on. With the children in a circle, choose one child to wear a monkey mask. Place some of the words in a basket and the corresponding rhyming word on the wall around the room. The 'monkey' picks a word from the basket, shows the rest of the class and goes off to find the word that rhymes with it. As he or she is hunting for the word the rest of the children chant "Monkey Do, Monkey Do, Monkey Do", until the word is found.

- The Queen of Rhyme (you in role) visits the class and invites the children to enter Rhymeland with her. Make a set of simple, rhyming picture cards. Place the cards on the board and invite two children at a time to find a rhyming pair and to stick them on to the Queen's dress.

## Practical Activities

- Play 'Monkey Monkey'. Make a set of laminated picture cards and place them around the hall or school. Each child needs a whiteboard, pen and a monkey mask. Wearing their monkey masks, the children go to each picture card, write the word on their whiteboard and a word that rhymes with it.

- Play 'Monkey Madness'. Make a set of large, rhyming picture or word cards. Cone off an area in the playground or hall. Half of the class wear a word on their backs and stand in the middle of the area. The other half stand around the edge holding a corresponding rhyming card. When the teacher says, "Monkey Madness!" the children around the edge chase the children in the centre and try to take the word that rhymes with their card.

- Play 'Royal Rhymes'. Make a set of rhyming picture cards and a set of large laminated cards with a picture of the 'Queen of Rhyme' on each. Children take turns to pick two cards from the bag. If the cards rhyme they place them on the Queen.

## Art and Display

- Paint and collage a large monkey and crocodile for the display. Add some rhyming words and the children's own monkey pictures

- Make monkey masks.

- Using watercolour pencils, design a new front cover for *Monkey Do*.

## Cross-curricular Links

- **ICT** – Turn a programmable robot into a crocodile. Program the crocodile to follow a route to locate the toy monkey.

- **PSHE** – Discuss with children the issue of keeping monkeys in captivity.

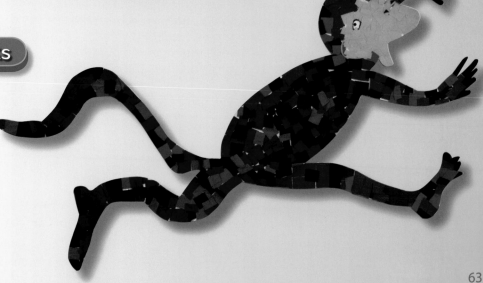

# Going on a Bear Hunt

## Whole-class Starter

- Read *We're Going on a Bear Hunt* by Michael Rosen and Helen Oxenbury (Walker Books). Ask the children to listen carefully to words such as 'SPLISH SPLASH' and 'SWISHY SWOSHY', and to guess what these words are trying to describe. Explain that these words use 'onomatopoeia' – they sound like their meaning. Maybe 'onomatopoeia' could become the weekly challenge word for spelling!

- Listen to a tape of different sounds, such as water running, a clock ticking, a drum beat etc. Ask the children to think of words to describe each sound.

- Make pairs of cards with pictures on one card and the corresponding sound in words on the other, for example, a picture of tap on one card and the words 'drip, drip, drop' on the other; a picture of a bag of crisps and the words 'crunch, crunch, crackle' and so on. (There should be one card for each child.) Give each child a card and, on the words "We're going on a sound hunt!", the children should form the correct pairs. Ask each pair to perform their sound!

## Practical Activities

- Make a story wheel called 'We're Going on a Bear Hunt' (see picture). Ask the children to write the onomatopoeic words in each section on the wheel.

### Focus of Learning

Looking at onomatopoeia

My Bear Hunt Story Wheel.

- Play 'Beware the Bear'. Make a large board game for six players. On the board include pictures such as a tap dripping, a bell ringing, a kettle boiling, a baby crying etc. At one end of the board is the bear cave and at the other end is the house. The object of the game is to get to the bear cave. Make a dice showing the numbers 1 to 5 plus a picture of a bear. Each child takes a turn and if they throw a bear they go back to the beginning. If they land on a picture they have to write the onomatopoeic word on a whiteboard.

- Using the same story format as *We're Going on a Bear Hunt* ask the children to make up their own version. For example, 'We're Going on a Beach Trip', or 'We're Going on a Picnic'.

## Art and Display

- Draw and pastel pictures of characters from the front cover of the book for display. Add onomatopoeic words.

- Paint and collage giant bears.

- Make bear finger puppets.

## Cross-curricular Links

- **GEOGRAPHY** – Draw a map of the story.

- **ICT** – Use a paint package to draw bears.

- **DRAMA/MUSIC** – Re-enact the story and use percussion to highlight the onomatopoeia.

- **PSHE** – Discuss the bear's feelings at the end of the story. Write a letter to the bear expressing views on his behaviour.

# Fidgety Fish

Fidgety Fish
alliteration

fiddly fish | favourite fish | fabulous fish
Try to alliterate your name! | funny fish
furious fish | fantastic fish | famous fish | fearful fish
fat fish | funky fish
fine fish | feminine fish

## Whole-class Starter

- Read the story *Fidgety Fish* by Ruth Galloway (Little Tiger Press) and discuss the title. Talk about 'alliteration' and ask the children to alliterate their own name.

- Play 'Under the Ocean I Saw …' with the children sitting in a circle. The first child says, for example, "Under the ocean I saw a shiny shark." The next child says, "Under the ocean I saw a shiny shark and a stunning starfish" and so on.

## Practical Activities

- Play 'Beat the Burp'. Make a set of ten fish-shaped, coloured cards. On seven cards write the word 'fish' and on the other three write the word 'BURP'. Make each child a laminated board with six fish shapes on it. Children take turns to pick a card from a blue bowl or bucket. If they pick a 'fish' card they write an alliterative word on one fish on their board, for example, 'funny fish', 'fat fish' and so on. If the child picks a 'BURP' card he or she rubs all his alliterative words off his or her board. The objective of the game is to be the first to fill the board.

## Focus of Learning

Understanding alliteration

- Play 'Fidgety Fishing'. Make a set of sea creatures and place them in a small paddling pool or water tray (with water in!). Give each child a fishing net. When they catch a creature they have to alliterate it.

- Using the title of the book as a stimulus, ask the children to create their own stories, such as 'Furious Fish', 'Fat Fish', 'Funny Fish'.

## Art and Display

- Make giant colourful pictures of a selection of characters from the story, such as jellyfish, limpets, crab. Display them on the board and ask the children to think of some alliterative adjectives, for example, 'jolly jellyfish', 'lucky limpet', 'crazy crab'. Add these to the display.

- Make papier mâché fish and hang these from the classroom ceiling.

- Use fish-shaped binca material to create a pattern using brightly coloured threads and felt. Alternatively, sew a fish shape onto blue hessian using silver thread. Add felt scales.

- Make clay fish shapes. Add detail by pressing different small shapes into the clay. Paint with pearlised paint.

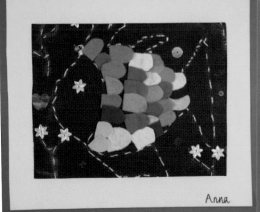

## Cross-curricular Links

- **ICT** – Use a paint package to create a fishy character.

- **SCIENCE** – Classify different kinds of fish using information books.

- **MATHS** – Create Carroll or Venn diagrams relating to sea life.

- **GEOGRAPHY** – On a world map locate different places where fish live.

# Haunted House

- In role as the Riddler speak to the children in riddles! (Base your costume on the Riddler from the Batman films). The Riddler says, "I am the Riddler, I speak in clues. How you use them you must choose. Listen carefully to what I say, then you will guess my riddles today". The Riddler puts one riddle at a time on the board and asks the children to work in pairs to work out the answer.

- Play 'Spin a Riddle'. On a spinner put pictures of interesting objects such as an apple, flower, bee, bell, house, skeleton, key and so on. Make a set of riddle cards which match the objects on the spinner. For example, 'I don't make wails, I don't make moans, I just rattle, I'm just bones' would be the riddle for the word 'skeleton'. The children sit in a circle and take turns to spin the spinner. The child then tries to find the correct riddle for the picture shown.

## Practical Activities

- Write a 'Haunted House' riddle. Make each child a haunted house-shaped book to write in.

- Play 'Ring a Riddle'. The children play against each other in pairs. Make a variety of riddle cards. Pairs of children should sit opposite each other, and each should have a card, a whiteboard and a pen. Place a small bell between each pair of children. Give each child a riddle card and, on a given signal, they read their riddle, write down what they think the answer is and ring the bell! This game could also be played as a small group circle game.

## Focus of Learning

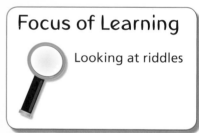

Looking at riddles

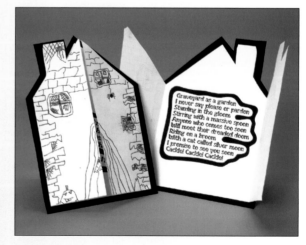

68

Down in the kitchen there's a funny smell.
Plop, fizz, bubble.
Is it a spell?
Yes, it'll make you sneeze and itch.
But who is the cook?
it must be a .....

- Play 'Reveal the Riddle'. Make a set of haunted house-shaped bingo boards with pictures on, such as a skeleton, a witch, a cobweb, a ghost, a bat, a spider and so on. Make a set of cobweb-shaped riddle cards and several Riddler cards (blank cards with a picture of the Riddler on). The children take turns to pick a card, read the riddle and match it to the picture on their board. If they pick a Riddler card they must remove all the riddles from their board.

## Art and Display

- Use paint and collage to make a display. Include a large vampire, ghost or Riddler, words related to haunted houses such as 'spider', 'bat', 'ghost' and riddles written by yourself or the children.

- Trickle PVA glue onto calico material in a spider's web shape or house shape. Leave to dry and paint with fabric dye. Peel off the PVA glue to reveal the original shape.

- Make pop-up cards (see picture). Using black paper, show the children how to make simple folded pop-up cards. The pop-up shapes could include spiders or spooky doors. These could have further flaps cut into them. Decorate with light-coloured pastels or chalk. Adventurous children could be allowed to investigate paper engineering.

## Cross-curricular Links

- **HISTORY** – Discuss the use and origin of riddles ('King Lear, Shakespeare').

- **DESIGN & TECHNOLOGY** – Use recycled materials to design and make haunted houses based on the pop-up book *Haunted House* by Jan Pienkowski (Walker Books).

I am the Riddler I speak in clues,
how you use them you must choose,
Listen carefully to what I say,
then you will guess my riddles today!

# Poppies

## Whole-class Starter

- Look at poppies – real or use pictures. Use Georgia O'Keefe's painting as a stimulus. Give each child a real poppy or a picture of one and ask them to think of words to describe their poppy.

- Play 'Pass the Poppy'. With the children in a circle, they think of a word to describe a poppy as they pass it round. Write the words on the board for them to see.

## Focus of Learning

Writing acrostics

## Practical Activities

- Give each child a poppy-shaped piece of paper to play 'Paper Poppies'. The children each write the first 'P' of the acrostic such as 'Perfect poppies swaying in the breeze' or simply 'P is for poppy'. The children pass their paper poppy to the next person in the group and they all write the 'O' part of the acrostic. Carry on around the group until the acrostic is finished.

- Play 'Name Your Acrostic'. Place lots of letters in the middle of the table. Each child collects the letters to make his or her name and places them acrostic-style on a whiteboard. Play some gentle music and ask the children to write an acrostic poem about themselves. To extend this activity the children could choose a friend's name.